Santa's Short Suit SHRUNK

and Other Christmas Tongue Twisters

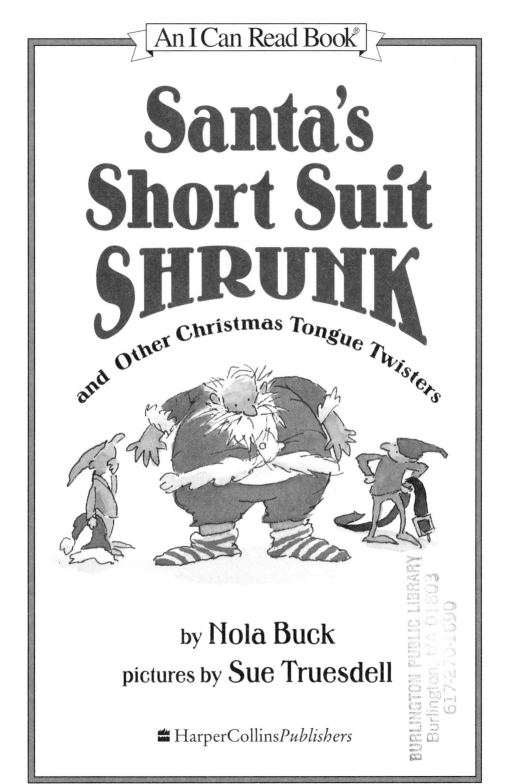

by Nola Buck

pictures by Sue Truesdell

HarperCollins*Publishers*

ER
BUCK

HarperCollins®, ✉®, and I Can Read Book®
are trademarks of HarperCollins Publishers Inc.

Santa's Short Suit Shrunk
And Other Christmas Tongue Twisters
Text copyright © 1997 by Nola Buck
Illustrations copyright © 1997 by Susan G. Truesdell
Printed in the U.S.A. All rights reserved.

Library of Congress Cataloging-in-Publication Data
Buck, Nola.
Santa's short suit shrunk and other Christmas tongue twisters / by Nola Buck ;
pictures by Sue Truesdell.
  p.   cm. — (An I can read book)
Summary: A collection of Christmas tongue twisters, including "Sarah
says she's sure she saw Santa" and "Greg gets Glenn a great green gift."
ISBN 0-06-026649-X. — ISBN 0-06-026663-5 (lib. bdg.)
1. Tongue twisters.   2. Christmas—Juvenile literature.   [1. Tongue
twisters.   2. Christmas.]   I. Truesdell, Sue, ill.   II. Title.   III. Series.
PN6371.5.B84   1997   96-29077
818'.5402—dc20   CIP
                                                                            AC

1   2   3   4   5   6   7   8   9   10
❖
First Edition

Visit us on the World Wide Web!
http://www.harperchildrens.com

For Nora
—N.B.

For Mom and Dad
with love
—S.T.

Six sick snowmen sniffle.

See Kate skate.

Skate, Kate, skate!

Bob borrows Barb's blue blanket.

Santa sees Sue's shoe shine sign,

so Sue shines Santa's shoes.

Bill buys Blair a big black bear.

BOOKS

TOYS

Sarah says she's sure she saw Santa.

Shy Sam Shaw saw the same Santa

Sarah says she saw.

These skis, please.

12

Is the Christmas shopping

stopping soon?

Greg gets Glenn a great green gift.

Bruce Black bought a blue spruce.

15

Blue bulbs blink.

Tinsel twine tangles.

Rhonda runs wild

with a wide red wreath.

Tall Tim trims thin twin trees.

Santa's short suit shrunk.

Wanda wraps with real red ribbon.

Sue shows Sally why she should share.

Bill's big bell bangs, *bing bam bong*.

Candy carries Carrie's candy cane.

A very merry Mary made the maid mad.

Nora lit the right white light.

Patty picks a pretty pleasant present.

Reindeer run over the red wet roof.

Santa stuffs some shocking stockings.

31

Sly Santa saw Sam Shaw sleeping.